Star CHILDREN

A Guide to Understand, Honor
and Empower the Star Child
Within and Around You

SHELLEY VECCHITTO

BALBOA.PRESS
A DIVISION OF HAY HOUSE

Balboa Press books may be ordered through booksellers or by contacting:

Balboa Press
A Division of Hay House
1663 Liberty Drive
Bloomington, IN 47403
www.balboapress.com
844-682-1282

Because of the dynamic nature of the Internet, any web addresses or links contained in this book may have changed since publication and may no longer be valid. The views expressed in this work are solely those of the author and do not necessarily reflect the views of the publisher, and the publisher hereby disclaims any responsibility for them.

The author of this book does not dispense medical advice or prescribe the use of any technique as a form of treatment for physical, emotional, or medical problems without the advice of a physician, either directly or indirectly. The intent of the author is only to offer information of a general nature to help you in your quest for emotional and spiritual well-being. In the event you use any of the information in this book for yourself, which is your constitutional right, the author and the publisher assume no responsibility for your actions.

Print information available on the last page.

ISBN: 978-1-9822-3083-8 (sc)
ISBN: 978-1-9822-4545-0 (hc)
ISBN: 978-1-9822-3090-6 (e)

Library of Congress Control Number: 2019908946

Balboa Press rev. date: 08/19/2021

Dedicated to my son Sage Atlas, a wise soul that came in and asked me to write the book before you. Deep loving gratitude to Luca, Star, Sun and all of the babies yet to come. My teachers, loves and guiding lights on Earth. To the child that we all are, igniting the highest essence of our soul here and now.

CONTENTS

INTRODUCTION

This is a powerful time of great importance for adults, children, animals, earth, and the light that we all are. You are being asked to create your own world, listen to the big call within your heart, remember why you are here, unite as love, and lift one another up. We are all miracles. Let's remember the power of love.

Truth is a joyful and expansive process. It comes with ease, smiles, and love—and sometimes tears, sadness, and release—as we discover and let go of old ways that once created our perceptions and ruled our lives. The path of discovery lifts everyone; it ripples to those you love, care for, and are connected to. Your realizations impact society and the interdimensional world in which we exist.

Saying *yes* to you on this beautiful journey is the most incredible experience. It is no secret that children remind us of our gifts and our truth and bring us back to our highest alignment here on earth. Children's clear vibrational energy exposes all of the stories within our hearts and souls that hold us back, bringing these to the surface so we can be free, move forward as who we truly are, and shed expectations, limitations, and fears from our consciousness.

Children remind us that we are children. Deep within each of us lives our inner child. This innocent, pure, creative, excited, delicate part of us desires to be heard, freed, loved, and connected.

This book invites you to explore what your inner child yearns for, and it opens a path in which you can connect and heal yourself.

You may wonder who the Star Children are and why it's important to bring light to their presence on earth. Let me share something big: you are a Star Child. Many of us completely dissociate energetically with our magical star frequency, while others remain activated in their star vibrancy. In this book, we will tune deeply into the activated Star Children. These souls are sensitive, emotional, connected, and unique. They are labeled as ADD/ADHD, autistic, different, or strong-willed. They show up with cancer, illness, or dis-ease. They bring messages of love, strength, and peace, invoking a deep invitation to go beyond your beliefs, to embrace something greater. They awaken, within your core, truth, wholeness, and an authentic remembering of who you are and why you are here.

Life as a gifted Star Child can be amazing; it can also be challenging. It is extremely powerful to acknowledge your children's gifts as well as your own. This is the first step to living a fulfilling, happy life as the unique and special soul you are and always have been. Your gifts and the children's gifts allow you to be an open vessel for healing, transformation and fulfillment. Just by being you and following your truth, you give others permission to do the same.

In the following chapters you will tap into your truth, feel your deepest desires, clear fears or stories as they appear, and activate in your highest essence. *Star Children* connects you with who you are while bringing awareness to today's children and their gifts, abilities, and purpose. It is a great honor to be here with you as you say yes to a happy life full of joy, love, peace, expansion, and adventure.

As you read these pages, your awareness will shift. You will experience clarity, healing, and insight and receive ideas that show you how to move forward from this point. It is truly a blessing to be on this path. I congratulate you for being open to exploring beyond your current perspective, and I welcome you with a gigantic soul smile and wide-open, happy heart on a path of abundance, peace, joy, freedom, and love.

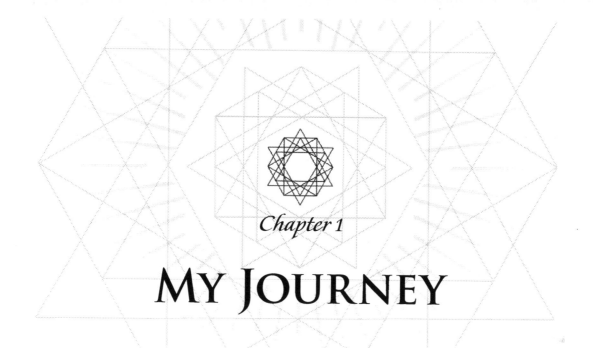

Chapter 1

MY JOURNEY

It began with me, a child born on planet Earth, here to experience the magical mysteries and flower-filled fields that live so vividly within my heart and soul. I know I am here as a great being of love, a miracle maker, a visionary, a healer, a conduit of pure energy, a voice for my highest self, and a creator of joy. When I entered this world as a small child, I remembered why I was here—living, breathing, and being me and then I forgot. I was lost in the experience of the life I was born into—the stories, expectations, and emotions and what was a wave of confusion for many years.

I felt deeply, cried rivers, played freely, and became a silent prisoner of the world I lived in. Trying to keep the peace that flowed so naturally within my soul, I found joy in the silent company of my companion kitties and the soft escape of worlds I discovered in books, sitting by rivers, and while resting under trees. I loved the forest, plants, animals, and star-filled skies. Everything else was just there, and I discovered ways to be happy. Yet deep inside, I was lost; something was missing. What could it be? It was me. I was disconnected from myself. This took years—a journey of many moons—to discover and was a continual journey of releasing the layers that are not authentically who I am. Today I sit here, grateful, humbled, radiantly loving this experience, its gifts and blessings, and the constant invitation to surrender deeply, open wide, and to live wildly free.

I am an angel on earth. I see, love, and know the best in all, with a deep desire to keep the peace, be loved, and love all into their wholeness. We choose our paths before we arrive on earth; this includes our missions, purposes, and families.

I grew up safe in a small rural community in Connecticut, on the East Coast of the United States. My parents divorced when I was four, and my mom and stepdad primarily raised me, with the exception of every-other-weekend visits with my dad and soon-to-be stepmom. My family followed traditional Catholic values, which were passed on from their upbringing. We were quiet on the outside, living very sheltered, ordinary lives. Yet my heart was broken by the stiffening silence. I could feel the pain, and it stirred deep within my soul. I cried the tears my loved ones held back and felt the pain buried deep in their hearts, completely unaware that this was something I was doing until much later in life.

My heart was broken by the collective wounds that many of us adopt merely by coming into a human body on earth at this time. The invitation to conform grew strong, yet the truth is my soul could only forget so much before I rebelled. I rebelled against my family and all that felt like a journey of numbness. As I entered middle school and chose my own friends, I realized that the limited perspective of my conservative upbringing and sheltered family life did not resonate with me; it was not my truth. My new friends made me aware that I was the peacekeeper, always apologizing and not understanding the worth of my words or perspective. They actively reminded me to stop apologizing; there was nothing to apologize for.

At age thirteen, I moved into a friend's home for a time, as the strict rules, ideas, and environment at home were stifling. At this time, I began dressing expressively, with angel-like clothes and often a head of tiny blonde braids. I began to explore drugs at the same time to numb all my uncomfortable feelings and gifts. It took the edge off while I came out of a sheltered closet, and it served as a means of self-exploration until I had the sudden realization that I was hurting myself. I went through this phase at a very young age and never had the desire to return to it, as it became a coping behavior. In reality, no one could stop me but, of course, myself.

When I finished high school, I knew it was time for change. I still was consumed by the ideas and limited perspective of society when I went to college. At this time, I was compelled by a force bigger than myself to move from Connecticut to Hawaii; I was starting fresh and felt fully invigorated by the magical energy of the islands. There were great changes and openings from within, as I obtained both a premedical and nursing bachelor's degree over eight years. Still only dabbling in my soul potential, I was lost and searching deeply for the reason I was here on earth. I asked myself how I was meant to serve.

My original intention was to become a naturopathic doctor and acupuncturist. My oldest angel child, Luca, was born just a week before I graduated with a premedical degree. I decided, for financial security, to study nursing. The years that followed showed me it was time to say goodbye to the ideas of living inside the box. I dug deep with all my heart and soul. I felt, cried, healed, listened to my heart, and began to unite with who I truly am. This deeply heartfelt journey was initiated by my eagerness to know and embrace myself, to remember my gifts and nurture them to the surface. I could feel. It was exciting and liberating, and it fed my soul. Finally, things were making sense in a way that made no sense at all.

Called forth by the deep ache in my soul to be alive, the first major event that inspired me to action was my guide, teacher, and friend, Koa, a four-legged furry creature who is a cat. A month after adopting this most exquisite orange ball of love, he became ill—paralyzed, seizing, and unable to manage bodily functions such as regulating his temperature, walking, eating, and going to the bathroom. After a week at the vet with no diagnosis or change, the only option they offered was to euthanize, but this was not an option to me—to give up on my baby. I took him home and nursed him back to health. Something bigger than me came through in those moments. It was my authentic ability to see him as healed, knowing, believing, and holding him in a space of divine perfection. This was the first taste of my true soul-calling in action.

At this time, a beautiful friend and mentor, who would work with Koa on an energetic spiritual level to heal, entered my life. I was blessed to study alongside this beautiful soul named Wendi. It happened magically and, as some would say, synchronistic. At the same time that I was called from deep within to learn meditation, I crossed paths with Wendi in our local health food store and was immediately inspired to ask whether I could study meditation with her. Several days later, she offered a unique one-on-one Reiki course. I said yes, knowing that this was divinely placed on my path, and I began a journey of connecting with the wisdom of my soul. In essence, it was not Reiki but something so much more. I connected with my ability to move energy, to be still, to be receptive, to surrender, and to receive the answers of the divine. This is when I began consciously receiving from spirit and healing my soul by removing masks and identities that were not my authentic soul essence. I opened to my gift of connecting with people who have left the physical realm through death. I could now clearly see beyond the layers that fellow humans wear, and was able to assist them in connecting with their highest essence, by inviting them into a space of opening deep within, releasing wounds, igniting wholeness, and living a life of authentic creative expression, freedom, and joy.

My soul smiled; my ability to see, connect, heal, radiate love, and be a vehicle of truth burst wide open. All the right teachers appeared at the perfect time, and I said yes to a flow of life that I had not known since my early youth. By the time I graduated from nursing school, I was living in alignment with spirit. It was clear I had to decide: would I become a nurse or venture off into the land of the unknown? This was a scary and liberating crossroad: to choose me or the false sense of stifling security that I was raised to believe was so important and almost vitally necessary to survive.

I chose me. And that is why we are sharing, expanding, loving, uniting, and healing here. I see you as who you really are and know that your greatness is unique, that your truth is one of a kind, and that you hold all of the answers within. You are here with a great purpose that only you can fulfill, and it's time for you to embrace this. If you have not received this message before now, I am sure the children in your life have given you many opportunities to open your heart and live.

I realized I am not on earth to assist people as a naturopathic doctor, acupuncturist, nurse, or even medical doctor. It was part of my journey to take this educational route in true form. It led me to finally discover myself and divinely activated my own journey of inner peace, healing, joy, and purpose.

The gifts within my soul speak loud and clear. I am a voice for the people, for you, for those who remember and are remembering who they are and why they are here. I am an advocate for the Star Children—a teacher, healer, psychic, medium, clairvoyant, telepath, and so much more magic than words can describe. My gifts go far beyond the words on this page, but I live in a human body, as do you, and I am ever so grateful to be on this journey of sharing, caring, and supporting one another.

In the pages that follow, I have completely let go and allowed spirit to guide this one-of-a-kind inspirational journey for you and the special child in your life.

Chapter 2

UNDERSTANDING YOUR CHILD

We are all the same on the deepest core level. You, me, the child next door—we all come from the same source energy of love. Along the way, our stories—the ones we were born carrying, told, and chose to take on as our own—began to shape the way we experience and live our lives.

How we understand and relate to our children can be blurred because of the circumstances of our lives, beliefs, and ways of operating in the world that we have adopted. The stories that you live are not necessarily pure truth; they are merely the reflection of everything you have heard and chose to think. It is now time to say goodbye to the stories, recognizing and thanking them for supporting you when they did. There is great power as you do this energetically; by claiming this, you offer them a beautiful resting place full of love and forgiveness and create space to say hello to who you truly are.

The key to understanding all of the beautiful souls here on earth is to keep in mind that as human beings, we tend to become bogged down with ideas, expectations, and demands from family, friends, school, society, or our own personal egos. This often leads us down a road of disconnection from our true essence, purpose, and inner joy.

The children who have chosen to be here today as your biological kids, students, grandchildren, nieces, nephews, neighbors, and more have come to wake you up. They have come with a very important mission. I am one of these children, and waking up to who I am has completely changed my experience. Things are so easy now that I understand why I am here. The most important thing we can do while we are here is to discover ourselves—our joy, passion, enthusiasm, sense of freedom, bliss, and excitement. When we experience these things, we are on the right path.

The children who have chosen to be here in your experience need one big thing from you—love. Your children need to feel safe in your arms, accepted exactly as they are, and supported in their unique expression as they grow, expand, and learn. They need to know that you are available with an open heart, no matter what has happened. You are the children's greatest provider of love, support, safety, and comfort in the world, beyond their personal connection to Source which can be defined as the purest form of energy that runs through all living things.

It is what you teach, believe, share, and experience that leads them forward on their earthly journey. In the end, you will realize that you called the children into your life just as much as they chose to be here with you.

Chapter 3

WHY THE NEW CHILDREN ARE NEEDED

Everyone on earth has a purpose. Adults, children, elders, animals, and even the trees are each on a mission. We are all here on earth to open our hearts, remember our magic, lift humanity up, and make a difference in the world. Along the way, we have experiences and adventures; our hearts feel excitement, joy, bliss, sadness, and confusion. We learn from family, peers, and society that acting a certain way seems to equal happiness. Many of us simply want to be accepted and welcomed with approval, appreciation, and unconditional love. In the midst of these experiences, we are frightened and just want to fit in. The world we are part of becomes the big picture. We no longer remember the core foundation of our existence and that we come bearing many inner-soul treasures.

As awakened, gifted souls, we are voices of truth. Our gifts and soul purposes make us unique and different, unable to fit and operate in the daily world in which many of us have grown up. Many unconsciously decide it is easier to close the door to their gifts, to simply say no from within, and to stop experiencing the unique, powerful soul essence that trembles within. Many humans are not aware that challenges show up because they are indeed very special. I am here telling you that moments which feel hard are blessings placed on your path by the divine as an invitation to dig deep within and remember your soul music.

It is our choice. We are the ones who decide how to live. If something creates more discomfort than joy, it makes sense to turn away from it. This is what many have done—chosen the path of least resistance. Yet in so doing, they have lost touch with a big part of their unique essence—the calling that brought them to earth, the magic that is them, which they are meant to share proudly.

The voice within you, the deep knowing of truth, the gifts your specific unique soul essence came to Earth to share needs to be honored, explored and deeply felt by you. As you move through honoring your voice there is a great big energetic wave of truth that flows out of you, it can be felt and seen thus you become medicine awakening others to remember their powerful mission, and the ripple goes onward.

Now the Star Children in our lives are here to wake us up. They are *big* examples of truth. Their work is to lift the layer of amnesia that has covered many of our souls and to remind us of who we truly are. They are healers, teachers, and miracles of love, joy, peace, and freedom. As we see their magic, freedom, and joy, we remember our own. They are us, and we are them.

Chapter 4

GETTING TO KNOW YOURSELF

There are many ways of looking at the children. In a way, it is like looking at yourself in the mirror. What is it about your child that you try to change, control, or fight? Our children are great reflections.

Have you ever tried to love that to which you are so reactive? This requires you to stop and breathe. Connect with your highest self, let go of the mind, and just be in the peaceful calm that exists deep within. You are invited to do this on a deeper level in the journal activity at the end of this chapter. Now enjoy a deep breath, and with this breath, welcome freedom. Breathe deep within your heart and soul, touching that place that knows all is well and that this moment is a blessing. Rightfully claim your readiness to fully embrace and receive the magic here.

Now that you are open, clear, and listening, what is it that pulls your strings? What are the children showing you about life and the needs you have right now? Once you have allowed yourself to feel beyond, within the depths of your soul, the underlying reactive component will disappear. You are set free by claiming this and proclaiming your readiness to consciously heal. Thank your little ones for being such amazing teachers—because they are.

As parents, many times we unconsciously try to make our children what we want or expect them to be. This is something to which the Star Children are extremely resistant.

It can cause many disruptive interactions when parents attempt to cut their children off from having freedom of choice, which includes expression (how they dress, act, react, speak, think, listen, etc.). If you take action from the space of anger or the need to control, they will protest, and you will see this in the form of resistance, tantrums, outbursts, and possibly tears. The children know that you are not aligned and will automatically show you by creating an experience that cannot be ignored.

When children revolt, we often are being shown that we hold a belief that is no longer in alignment with truth. We are given an opportunity to seek clarity, recognize the source of the reaction, and release it into the universe with love, joy, and gratitude. This story no longer serves you in the highest good for all, and so it has come to the surface to be honored and freed. In the process, your consciousness is elevated, and you align with your true self, free of stories that once kept you safe from the vastness of truly living.

Recently, family was visiting, and I witnessed my dad—we like to call him Pa—whom I love and adore, treating the kids like he treated me as a child. I just sat back and observed, learning and taking it in from this new perspective. He had certain ideals, such as how long my oldest angel, Luca's, hair should be. I observed as Luca wanted to receive Pa's approval and took part in the change, yet within Luca loved the way he was. I also saw my youngest angel, Sage Atlas, listen to Pa when he was stern, yet when the sternness switched to controlling, he revolted and ran to me. Take note when your children are not listening. Look deeper, going beyond the surface. Let go of your ego and expectations, and you will clearly see what your children are showing you.

This is a very important topic, as the expectations we put on our children can cause them to shut down their gifts and dim their natural essence in order to please us and receive the love and acceptance we all seek as human beings. You may have experienced this during your lifetime. I know that I have. It is easy and joyful to clearly see when we are ready to let go and heal deeply. Sometimes it takes a major illness or emotional breakdown for us to seek the messages available from within. Once we heal from this space, everything in our lives lines up, and we open to receive love, peace, joy, harmony, and abundance. The path is always perfect; no matter what happens, every piece of the journey leads to new realizations, opportunities, and greater awareness. Be proud of who you are, where you have been, and all of the incredible things you have taken on as a human being.

Here is a journal activity that invites you to enjoy a moment of clarity
as you receive guidance, joy, and abundance from within.

Journal Activity

Take out your journal and create a peaceful place to sit and reflect. You may play quiet, calming music; light a candle; dim the lights; or sit on the grass. Do exactly what you are guided to do.

Once you are in your peaceful space, close your eyes and breathe. Call in your highest self, your angels, ascended masters, Source, and any beings in the nonphysical realm to which you feel connected in this moment to bring clarity and healing and allow you to see transparently.

Set an intention (a desire or what you wish to call in, understand or create).

Breathe until you feel clean, clear, and light inside.

Open your journal and begin writing. You will write what comes through you. The purpose is to connect and receive divine guidance, so trust and allow.

When you are finished writing, take a moment to thank all of the divine beings in spirit for their assistance, send them love, and let them go. Be sure to thank yourself for being present and willing too.

Once again, close your eyes and breathe until you feel complete, full, and whole as the love and light that you are.

Chapter 5

WHERE STAR CHILDREN COME FROM

T he new children come from various star planets. These planets have been watching earth for quite some time and are on a mission to help restore and save our planet from self-destruction. After quite some time, it became clear to these planets that watch over the progress on earth that it was necessary to send large numbers of souls in order to create change. Each Star Child signed up to accomplish a specific mission. Now there are big waves of Star Children coming. This is because what has been witnessed on earth in the past ten years shows that in order to create a big wave of change, which is imminent for earth, an abundance of the magical energy the Star Children exude must be potently available so that earth can thrive.

On their home star planets, all of the new children are powerful light beings. Many planets rely primarily on telepathic communication. Most souls can teleport in a moment wherever they need to be. Energy can be shifted, and healing as well as alignment happens instantaneously. The lands are lush and magical. The community is united in love; everyone gets along and honors all life. There is no need to eat, as the energetic body is always tapped in and nourished. Life is fun and magical.

When a Star Child arrives on earth, the change in vibration is intense, as is the experience for them. This is why the new children arrive on earth in steps; for example, perhaps Mom miscarries but then has a successful pregnancy. Often it is necessary for powerful new children to integrate in steps. (I speak in greater detail about this in chapter 13, "Miscarriage.")

We will see that these children do not need to hide their gifts, and the ones who are born now will have capabilities similar to those they experienced on their star planet. In the past, if they came in with these powerful gifts, society would have labeled and institutionalized them. We have come to a turning point where the gifts will be recognized as special, and so this makes it safe for the children to start integrating with these high-potency abilities, such as moving objects without touching them.

The Star Child's goal is to restore the frequency of love here on earth, to heal the land, to remind humans of their unique purpose and personal gifts, and to activate a deep, conscious connection within all forms of life. Their high vibrational presence is creating a purging right now that will last for several years. This is a release of old ideas, ways of being, and toxic patterns that hurt humans as well as Mother Earth. Just as a volcano erupts and a new land is birthed, the old toxic energy must be released for new energy to emerge.

The new children of all ages are here to anchor love, even under the most chaotic of circumstances, always seeing the divine order and blessings in everything. This is a great part of their medicine on earth; they do not feed fear energy when living in alignment with their true purposes and earthly missions. A successful mission is one where the new children live lives of truth, remember who they are, honor their gifts, and ripple this frequency out in the world for others to do the same.

Chapter 6

THE STAR CHILDREN

Many of the children here and coming to earth have powerful gifts. They are here to make a difference; to remind us of who we are and why we are here; and to show the way by healing our minds, bodies, hearts, and spirits. They recognize the oneness between all living things, and their magical *knowing* transforms our consciousness and heals the earth quickly.

All the children on earth are Star Children, which makes you a Star Child too. The children of whom I speak are unique activated Star Children, with great big eyes, hearts that light the world, and spirits of unconditional love. They are labeled too often as having ADD/ADHD or autism. The new children are the ones with cancer or any type of illness. These children with big spirits don't always fit in because they are different, highly conscious, tuned in, and aware beings. They see spirit and are completely connected to Source. You may have looked into a child's eyes and felt the powerful presence, wisdom, and connection that these children share. It's exciting and brings a part of you to life that perhaps went dormant—a very magical, pure part of your soul.

You may wonder why the activated Star Children are flooding the planet at this time. They have been called in to restore health, happiness, balance, and peace. A major shift in consciousness is necessary to restore harmony and joy. This is due to the energy of domination that has been at the forefront of society for some time. The activated Star Children laugh in the face of such things. They know, deep within, that they are free with choices, voices, and a new, inspiring way. They bring forth community, love, laughter, and abundance in its purest form.

Are you a Star Child? Yes. You came across this book because you are a Star Child. This was written to remind you of who you are. Not all adults are activated Star Children, but many are. Activated Star Children are defined as highly conscious souls that came to earth with a mission of living in full alignment with their highest selves, to remind others of their purpose, to heal the planet, and to awaken an experience of pure unconditional love. You don't need to remember who you are to be a Star Child. When you do awaken to this truth, life will become clear, happy, aligned, and very magical—that is what we refer to as an activated Star Child.

I can vouch for this experience. My life changed completely upon realizing I am a Crystal Child- a star child with a specific set of general characteristics (see the detailed description of various types of star children in chapter 8). Suddenly, everything made sense—all of my experiences, visions, what makes my heart sing. The biggest part was receiving confirmation of why I am alive. My life path is not an option that could be discovered or claimed within a college education, career path, or job. When I realized I was here to create my own way, to live my truth, and to serve as a loving messenger and example for others to do the same, my entire world lit up. I had great magical wings, and my dreams suddenly had permission to become my reality. In an instant, I could breathe easily, smile, sparkle, and be myself.

I have been called to honor the activated Star Children and educate the planet because often they are misunderstood, labeled, and not recognized for the amazing blessings that they are. I am a voice for you and the children. Today, I ask you to put aside everything you think about yourself—what is right, wrong, or not appropriate. I welcome you on this incredible voyage and thank you for being here.

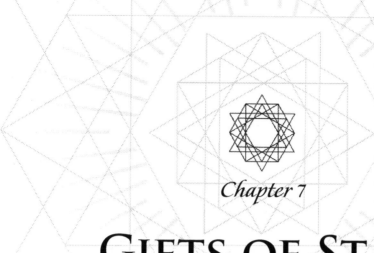

Chapter 7

GIFTS OF STAR CHILDREN

I t is important to be conscious of the children's gifts and the effects these have on their earthly experience, for their presence is rippling renewal, happiness, peace, and well-being. The activated Star Children have many characteristics in common. They hold individual intelligences, offering their personal gifts, realizations, healing ways, and special essences.

Each activated Star Child has a unique set of gifts. One child may express all the gifts mentioned in this chapter; another may have a strong psychic ability; some are powerful in multiple areas. We are all different. You have some of these gifts too. Tune in as you read, and see what resonates. I welcome you on this joyful path of enlightened self-discovery and expansiveness.

Psychic Abilities

Psychic children know things before they happen. They foresee the future. The means of their messages vary; some receive insight in dreams and others through words, feelings, or visions. It may be overwhelming for children, as well as adults, who have a sudden onset of these experiences. Sometimes psychic gifts are suppressed due to fear, emotional trauma, or simply because they are not used. This can protect and shield as well as make it easier to experience life on earth, simply by fitting in with the majority of humans. Likewise, psychic abilities can be activated by the deep desire to connect with one's true essence, by visiting a sacred spiritual place, consciously healing the emotional energetic shields acquired over time, or through an unexpected awakening or near-death experience.

Here is what Shana, a radiant, loving mom, witnessed in a dream, which called her into action. In her dream, Shana saw her eight-year-old son, Jamie, who was spending the night with a friend, get into a white van and head to the beach. On the way, the van was in an accident, and no one survived. Her dream felt far-fetched since, to Shana's knowledge, the family did not own a white van, but she was so shaken when she awoke that she picked up the phone to warn them. To her surprise, she learned that the family had bought a white van the night before and were about the head out on a long, winding drive to the beach on the exact road she'd seen in her dream. To this day, Shana is thankful she followed her instincts and called, possibly saving the family from a huge tragedy.

Psychic ability is a very powerful gift to have. The message for you, regarding the children in your life and even yourself, is to live with an open mind and listen with your whole heart. When kids confide and share premonitions, dreams, or ideas with you, be present. Many may feel these stories are fantasy, but in reality, children live in many realms, not just on earth. They are very connected and in tune. It benefits everyone when we take time to connect, listen, and invite others to expand on their ideas, thoughts, feelings, and experiences. Have you had such aligned and awakening experiences and premonitions yourself? Perhaps you too have a psychic gift.

Empathy

For an empathic human, the world can be an overwhelming place. There are so many emotions to experience that sensitive souls often feel lost, confused, and overwhelmed. This is because they feel the emotional experiences of many. Simply passing by someone can bring on an intense onset of emotions, physical sensations, or realizations. Sensitive or empathic people crave time in solitude, in nature, or near water. They require regular energetic cleansing, as well as connecting routines, such as meditation, to live in harmony.

I ran a half marathon several years ago. Running is fun for me, and I enjoyed the energy of the race. There were so many people that in order to keep a flowing pace, I had to pass runners—this was when I started to pick up on different physical pains in my body. As I passed one runner, my stomach hurt; then it was my knee, neck, or a sudden stitch. I quickly realized I was feeling the pain of people as I passed them. It was quite a journey. It helped when I recognized what was occurring; it empowered me to realize the pains weren't mine, which allowed each experience to quickly disappear.

Empathy is a gift that allows you to assist people who are not tuned in to their intuitive, physical, emotional bodies. When you have the gift of empathy, you are able to reveal clearly what another has been suppressing so that it can be loved and freed. We all want to live happy, joyful, abundant lives, and this awareness allows for just that.

Children are highly empathic. They detect your emotions, needs, and desires without the need for words, and they offer you support before you're even aware of it. Children are true angels in our lives.

Intuition

To be intuitive is to have a *knowing*. We are all intuitive beings. The level to which we trust, invite, and activate this divine gift differs from person to person. You choose to open your intuitive experience by allowing nudges, messages, and guidance to lead you forward in life. This is a powerful practice. Receiving magical messages and intuitive guidance from the universe will change your life. It is important to encourage children to tap into their intuition. Ask them how they feel about something, and trust that they know—because they do. When you live based on your intuitive knowing, the flow of greatness you will experience is amazing.

Children are born completely tapped in to this power. They can teach a lot when you honor their perspectives and listen with your heart. Let them show you the way in this life, instead of teaching them what you have learned. They hold great wisdom and purity. This is why they are here in your life—to remind you of truth and to guide you home to who you really are.

I invite you to allow your intuition to guide you today. Follow the inner voice that speaks to you. The deep knowing is there all of the time; all you have to do is listen. Perhaps you are guided to go somewhere on a whim that makes no sense. Say yes to this. I promise you that magic will happen when you allow yourself to follow a path guided by spirit.

I follow that inner voice and trust it. One day I was guided to go to a temple down the street from my home. The guidance was clear and urgent, so I got in the car with my newborn, and we drove to the temple. It was surrounded by a beautiful garden with many sitting areas and things to enjoy. As we approached the altar, a man was standing at the door, speaking to a young girl, who appeared to be around six years old; she was with her parents and grandmother. I stood at the door, waiting for our time to enter, and I heard the gentleman ask the young girl whether she was an only child. She said no and explained that her older sister, who was eleven, had died yesterday.

Her family then shared that they'd come to the temple because this was where their daughter, who just had transitioned to spirit, wanted to go. They were on vacation, and she had unexpectedly had an allergic reaction to a medication and did not survive. Their daughter was present in spirit. She called me to be there to serve as a medium who could relay healing messages and connect her with her family in a very physical way at this pivotal moment. This is a powerful example of how we are guided by something higher then ourselves. Trust it, and say yes. It usually makes no sense to the mind, but you must just trust.

As you trust and honor this within your child, you will realize that you too have the gift of intuition. Ask, listen, and take action.

Mediumship

Activated Star Children have the gift of seeing and communicating with souls that have passed on from the physical realm. This is often referred to as mediumship. When you or your child sees, hears, or senses a soul that left a physical body, know this is very normal and completely safe. There are beings all around us all the time. Connecting with spirits is a normal, everyday occurrence for Star Children, who are experiencing their gifts and saying yes to their mission on earth.

It is empowering to talk to children about the realm of spirits that live among and beyond us. Children may have an "imaginary" friend, or they may say something like, "Grandma is here, and she told me …" This is because they are still in complete connection with who they really are, and they feel safe being their authentic selves in the world. When children talk about such experiences, they are sharing something very real. Listen with an open heart, and allow them to speak about the event. The more you allow them to feel safe as they connect, the more information and greater understanding they will receive about the experience. You too will expand in a new way through the process.

The following is about a special five-year-old girl named Savannah: When her family moved into a new home, she told her mom, Jackie, "Emma lives next door." Savannah had been seeing spirits since before she could speak, so her mom was accustomed to this and was open and interested. Jackie learned from listening to Savannah that Emma was two or three years old. It all came together one day when Jackie was walking through the cemetery next to their home. Before her was a grave for a young toddler named Emily. For Jackie, this was confirmation of her daughter's gift and the accuracy of what she was saying.

If you are a Star Child in an adult body, you may have the gift of mediumship as well. Do you remember hiding under the covers as a child because you feared monsters in the closet or you felt like there were people hiding under the bed? I do. This is what it feels like if we have this gift but fear it rather than expand it. As we spend time on earth but are never told about the existence and connection we all have with souls, including those who no longer live in physical bodies, such as angels, spirit guides, and loved ones who have transitioned, our souls can forget it is possible to see spirits or speak with them, so the light activation around this gift goes dim until something sparks it back to life. Another reason this gift often becomes hidden is to allow us to easily fit in, feel safe, and not stick out as being crazy, weird, or out of the ordinary. Gifted souls dim this gift or brush it off as being an imaginary, made-up experience that could not possibly be real. There is great power, joy, and relief in allowing yourself to "see" again.

Healing

You may wonder what it means to be a healer. Activated Star Children have the gift of healing in magical ways, which cannot be explained in scientific terms. This is because they have the ability to *see*. This is another sense with which we come to earth. All of our gifts combine when a healing occurs. This truly aligns you with your highest essence—the pure energy archetype that you were, long before you came to earth, and that you always will be in the highest vibration of existence.

This type of healing releases emotional, energetic bodies that you have been unconsciously holding on to. These aspects, if not released, can manifest as physical ailments, disease, emotional experiences, and relationship patterns. The healing that an activated Star Child initiates restores your cells to their natural state of equilibrium, balance, and integrity. It ripples as an awakening within the soul and serves as a catalyst, propelling changes in your perspective and welcoming new experiences here on earth. For instance, you may decide that your career, relationship, lifestyle or your way of thinking, operating, or experiencing life is no longer appealing, and so you seek joy, embrace love, and ultimately remember who you really are.

As a healer, I have the amazing and transformative ability to tap into the energetic body, soul essence, and spiritual source of who someone really is. I am gifted with the opportunity to lift old identifications that people have of themselves and who they are. I am able to heal wounds on an energetic, emotional, physical, and spiritual level, restoring the body and soul to its natural intelligence and vibrancy so that you remember who you are, and so you are fully connected with this on your earthly journey. What comes through me is exactly what each soul calls in; each experience is authentically different from the next. I love the magic that comes through. The shifts and healing are out of this world. Witnessing souls as they expand into their fullness, healing from dis-ease, saying yes to a life that is a full expression of who they are—this is why I am here. This is true healing, holding space for everyone to remember that within, they can heal themselves. Medically, I have assisted souls with stage-four cancer, blood clots, confusion, depression, and calcified organs; these souls have been restored to their complete wholeness with a session or two. This is because they are ready to heal on this very powerful level and activate the healer within, claiming their truth and being whole.

Telepathy

Telepathic communication requires no verbal words. Instead, the message travels from soul to soul as energy. This can be experienced as a *knowing* or feeling, as clear as any conversation with words.

We are all born with the gift of telepathy. Whether we use it or not determines the strength of this gift. Children are born into the world with this as their purest means of communication, for they have been using it since before they entered the womb and, of course, the entire time they were in utero. Many of the new children coming in choose to continue using this as their main form of communication.

Now you understand why there has been an influx in diagnoses of certain labeled "diseases" in which children do not communicate verbally, such as autism and Asperger's syndrome. They are gifted. There is no need to worry. They have chosen to be their authentic selves. Learn to listen to them and connect in other ways. I promise they will speak when and if they choose to speak. They are here to remind you that it is okay to be different and to teach you to go beyond what you perceive as limited and what you are told is "normal." There is no such thing as normal. When you truly accept your child and yourself as whole and perfect, you will transcend what you were once afraid of.

It is fun to expand your telepathic gift and to keep children in the flow of practicing with you. My son Luca and I communicate telepathically. We began consciously practicing when he entered kindergarten. I offered this idea to him: "Let's practice communicating without words. When you are ready to come home from aftercare, let me know by thinking it and setting the intention that I receive the message." I would check in consciously after school let out, and when I received the telepathic message, I would go to get him. This always worked wonderfully, and it is fun as well as empowering to connect in this very natural way.

You may realize that you also have telepathic experiences with close friends, loved ones, or children. It may come as a sense of reading someone's mind. Have fun playing with this and expanding your gifts.

Chapter 8

TYPES OF STAR CHILDREN

Here we explore the Indigo, Crystal, Rainbow, Dolphin, and Unicorn Children. I prefer to avoid labels, so in this case, take them lightly and allow them to empower you. In my experience, the identification of myself as a Crystal Child helped me to understand my earthly existence and gave me confirmation of why I had the experiences I did. It assisted me in recognizing my purpose and gave me the confidence to walk in a direction that was opposite the expectations of society and my family. I hope this information brings you peace, clarity, and direction. It is intended to empower and uplift you and the children in your life.

All Star Children are special. One is not better than the other. We each have a unique intelligence from which we operate. Exploring the various Star Children will empower you to deeply understand yourself and the children in your life. As you read, feel, and integrate the following chapters, invite your intuition to guide you and show you what is important for your personal experience.

Indigo Children

The Indigos are a generation of pioneers here on earth. They came to initiate change, bringing truth and clarity by taking action in politics, the workplace, within school systems, and at home. A telltale sign of Indigos is that they know when someone is speaking truth.

They are here to change the way we live and are doing major deconstructive work in society, ridding systems built on a foundation of greed, fear, and control. They are replacing these structures with evolved, heartfelt creations that lift and honor our true essence of love. The Indigo Children paved the pathway for the generations of gifted souls to follow.

These souls are wise beyond their years, with an energetic presence of power. They have an undeniable ability to detect truth. When falsehoods are present, they know deep within that something is not right. As with any gift, there are drawbacks; sometimes the Indigo Children dismiss their intuitive nudge to compensate and fulfill their innate need to be loved and accepted. This can lead to an unfulfilling experience for as long as the Indigo Children decide to hold on to the story and let go of their truth.

There are many opportunities for Indigos to reunite with their missions and true identities if they have veered away for any time. Synchronized opportunities will occur, such as meeting someone who reminds them of who they are, a physical illness, losing a loved one, the ending of a relationship, having a child of their own, or simply experiencing the desire for greater fulfillment. All of these scenarios are great blessings that open them to inquiring deep within, seeking answers, healing, and awakening their unique essences.

When an Indigo soul is reuniting with their true wholeness, they can experience deep emotions, anger, sadness, and a sense of isolation. Everyone does not welcome their direct approach or stubborn, outspoken way. They often lack the desire to withhold information, and sometimes their profound yet blunt insight makes others withdraw. This can lead to their feeling abandoned and cause the Indigo Child to forge forward independently.

The awake Indigo shines. They know who they are, and they live lives of incredible purpose. Their presence ripples far and wide, making a huge vibrational imprint wherever they are. It is the Indigo's gift to see truth. When one sees truth, they wake others to their own inner truths. This is a very beautiful and powerful offering.

The Indigo Children have a dark-blue aura, as noted in the name *indigo*. They also have a grounded presence and stand powerfully in their space. I see them as deeply rooted trees, lifting up those around them, providing a great foundation for all to flourish.

Crystal Children

Crystal Children are innately connected to the emotional body of all beings. They can feel clearly and are highly capable of assisting souls in releasing energy that has been stored through lifetimes, thus creating space for activation of the highest self, clarity, and alignment. Powerful healers by nature, these souls have a sweet, shining elegance to them.

Crystal Children are caring, sweet, gentle, genuine, honest, trustworthy, open, and easy to talk to. You may find that you pour out your deepest worries or intense experiences to these special souls. They are natural-born healers with very strong psychic, intuitive, medium, telepathic, and empathic abilities. Nature and animals are very close to their hearts, offering a safe, peaceful place to retreat and a joyful opportunity to connect deeply with themselves. Crystal Children are connected with the spirit realm and are highly aware of this when they are "awake."

Crystal Children are peacekeepers. They avoid conflict and listen with their hearts. These children are aware of experiences a soul may have had in this lifetime or others, as well as old stories that someone may be living. As natural healers, they magically assist in connecting souls with deep, hidden emotions and help to quickly clear things that no longer serve someone in the highest and best.

As highly empathic, sensitive souls, the Crystal Children tend to hold weight as a protective barrier from harsh energy. When they become aware of their gifts, it is easy for them to learn how to cleanse their energetic fields and stay connected to their own energy. This consciousness allows them to release the need for additional energetic protection, which results in weight loss and increased happiness. Most often, major life changes follow; for example, there can be a significant shift in their career choices, relationships, and how they view themselves and others.

Nature is a powerful resource for these beautiful souls. They are completely at home and connected when in natural settings, whether in a forest or a meadow, by a stream or the ocean. The peaceful environment and clear vibration of nature allows Crystal Children to easily connect with their true essence.

Animals are also a great source of peace for these children. There are several reasons for this. Crystals' ability to communicate telepathically creates a close relationship between them and animals. They innately know that animals are helpers that provide healing and trustworthy companionship and that lift their vibrations. Many Crystal Children do not eat animals, as they can feel the pain and suffering the animals have experienced. This deep understanding of the worthiness of all living beings shapes their experience.

As strong empaths, Crystal Children can feel overwhelmed in large crowds and may leave such settings feeling drained or emotionally overloaded. This is because they feel and experience what others in their vicinity are going through. For this reason, they enjoy time in solitude. They require this space to recharge and live harmonious, balanced, joyful lives.

Crystal Children are great teachers. They come from the heart and honor all souls, seeing the highest and best within them. The safe space they create allows others to explore who they are and often results in great clarity.

Rainbow Children

Rainbow Children heal our emotional bodies. They are highly empathic, passionate, loving, vibrant, joyful souls who love to talk and have immense psychic, telepathic, and energetic healing capabilities. Their hugs alone can open your soul so wide that it brings tears.

These children are the color of the rainbow. Their energy is high, fast, passionate, and loving. They're constantly on the move; this active nature helps them to maintain their high vibrational frequency, which shifts energy and keeps them connected to their own authentic soul vibrations. This joyfully explains why they don't know how to sit still. It is natural for them to be very active and intrigued, asking questions and more questions; of course, they are talkers.

These children are here to clear, uplift, and cleanse our emotional bodies. They know our truth and see us as pure love, as long as they feel safe and honored on this planet. The ways of the world do not always make sense to them. They know and expect everything to be pure, sparkling, perfect, and magical because in true form, it is.

The Rainbow Children are highly sensitive to the energy of those around them, their environment, and the food they consume. This affects the way they feel, act, and interact. It is important to teach them how to cleanse, protect, and tune in to their individual Source energy. This integration allows them to be grounded, happy, excited, alive, and abundant for their entire journey on earth.

Rainbow Children need to be heard. This is not merely listening with your head, but consciously tuning in to them with your heart and soul. They know the difference between heart and mind presence. When they realize you are not coming from love, they stop listening, and life will be a struggle until you accept that they are indeed teaching you. The lesson is this: you only get what you truly want when you move with love, faith, and trust from the sacred space of your heart.

It is equally important to give them space and time to connect in nature. They especially enjoy being in or near water. Water has a soothing effect on their souls. It activates their original vibration and releases anything that is not their highest essence. As mentioned earlier, they are empathic souls, so it is easy for them to take on emotions, thoughts, or ideas that are not theirs. For instance, when my son Luca was six years old, he would come home from school acting quite bossy. I was shown this behavior was due to the energy he experienced at school. In class, he was told what to do, with few to no options of making independent decisions.

When we picked him up, he was bossy with us, which was not his authentic vibration. We took note and offered him the opportunity to bathe in a lovely salt bath with essential oils. This is a daily practice for him after school and whenever he feels overwhelmed. It centers, calms, and opens him up to his highest essence. In the process, he has many realizations. This year, Luca has a new teacher. One day after starting with this new teacher, he came to me and said, "Mom, I can listen to my teacher this year because she comes from love. Last year my teacher was always yelling and mad." For children, or even for us, emotions may be triggered along our journey. It could be a song we heard, a classmate who brought up something, witnessing someone hurting another's feelings, or even an unknown reason. It is powerful for our children—and for us—to be in a loving, open space.

Rainbow Children enjoy helping people. It is part of their purpose to interact with and uplift the souls around them. They do this simply by being their bright, authentic, unique selves. These children don't care what others think of them. They act, say, and dress in ways that reflect their flamboyant, joyful inner space. This is a powerful aspect of who they are, and it must be honored. They teach us that it does not matter what others think; all that matters is being true to ourselves. For instance, if you ask them for suggestions on attire they will direct you toward something that makes you feel truly free and happy. The way we look on the outside often reflects how we feel within.

It is important to offer Rainbow Children space, time, and many opportunities to recharge and connect with themselves in solitude. This is important, as they are always "working." We become drained and lost if we are always helping others. Rainbow Children are the same in this respect. They require clearing, cleansing, and tuning in to be happy. This form of self-care is of utmost importance for the children of the rainbow vibration and you.

Their vibration shines, their smiles are as big as their faces, and they lift everything up with their energy when they are connected. Think about how you, as a parent or Rainbow, can help with maintaining this clear connection in life.

Dolphin Children

These exquisite beings have come to earth to remove the story from your existence. Their energy is pure, clean, and heaven-sent. The majority of these souls have not been to earth previously. They have a calm, angelic demeanor, and their eyes tell stories of their own. One glimpse, and they take you to another world, one free of worries, threats, and the need to understand the questions you ponder with your mind. The message they bring to the world is that everything is okay. There is no need for the excessive desire to control or understand. Instead, be free.

When a Dolphin Child enters your life, you will know it. Their presence allows all that is not aligned with your highest good to surface. The old stories that ruled your life, the things you saw as limits, and wounds that caused you heartache will be expunged in the most cleansing and purifying manner. They are here to assist you in letting go of the past so you can be fully present in the now. This is the gift of the Dolphin Child.

Charismatic, independent, loving, and quirky, these children rule the world with love, open hearts, and starlight energy of peace. They are here to raise the vibration of earth and to heal the planet.

The most important thing to understand about these vibrant souls is that they are sensitive beings. They can feel what is occurring energetically within you, your family, their peers, the community, and earth on a global scale. This is a gift, and it is beneficial to honor their gift by understanding the flux in their emotions. They are plugged into a sacred network and are always doing energetic work in the world, as well as within your soul. When your child experiences one of these moments, be aware. Create a moment to breathe, clear, and connect with your divine Source. The calm, peace, and awareness that your presence offers is a sacred portal of love that invites Dolphin Children to resume their connection with their divine Source and again experience balance. This can be playful and fun. It also serves to empower and align you. Perhaps the tantrum was a ripple of your energy.

Special Tips for Dolphin Children

- Water balances their spirits. Make sure to bathe them daily. You can add salts to the bath, as well as a loving intention. Take them to the ocean, river, lake, or stream. Make sure they stay hydrated.

- These children are highly telepathic and know what is going on without hearing about it verbally. They bring to the surface anything you need to let go of. Know that this is a great gift, and allow them to share. If they are upset or agitated, accept this as a cue to slow down and go within (for example breathe deeply, slow down, meditate), embrace the moment with presence, and ask, "What am I to recognize here?" Quickly, the situation will transform, and you will feel peace, harmony, and sweet tranquility.

- As highly receptive, sensitive souls, it is important for them to have plenty of access to nature, grass, clean air, animals, and water. This allows them to easily stay connected to Source and be at one with their purest, most balanced state. If you are in the city, then create a routine that allows you to frequent a local park; fill your home with plants or a water fountain; and purchase essential-oil mists to incorporate nature's grounding properties in your home.

- Learning is easy for these children. In an academic sense, they will be ahead of most other children, as their natural abilities allow them to absorb the information without having to read, hear, or memorize all of the details. They need more creative, playful expression, which may lead you to consider different options as they enter the school-age years.

- Food is best when it is clean, alive, and in its most natural state. These souls easily feel the effects of the food they consume. To keep their system running at a high vibrational frequency, buy fresh, locally produced, and organic food. Bless the food you eat with love; thank it. Cook as much as you can from scratch. This assures that you know the quality and creates a true connection between you, Mother Earth, your family, and the cycle of oneness. We are all here for one another. It's fun to involve your little ones in the creative cooking process. They will love this, and you both will benefit from the joyful time together.

Unicorn Children

The Unicorn Children are exquisite Buddhas. They hold the most amazing space of love, stillness, purity, and peace. I have only met a few of these souls; my son Sage Atlas is one of them. The Unicorn Children change the way we see ourselves and the world we live in, awakening us into the ease of being who we really are. They are like no other—sages, wise ones with eternal spirit energy that ripples far and wide.

It is easy for these children to stay balanced in their center. They are so incredibly connected to Source that when they help others, they are typically not affected. A great reason they experience this is that they always are in play mode, enjoying the moment, laughing, making jokes, and living.

The use of their light, playful energy brings you instantly into the moment. Everything falls away, and you are there with them in joy. I experience this with my son Sage all the time. When he was only a few months old, I was tearful one day. He came to me, looked deeply into my eyes, and laughed a big-belly, joyful laugh, with his presence saying, "Mom, life is good—remember." With that, I was back, present, smiling, and connected. I am so thankful for all of the angels that assist me on my journey, especially my children and loveable furry family.

As Unicorn Children grow older, they can take on the energy of those around them as their mission is to assist and expand. They will push boundaries and act as wild creatures of freedom. They will use limited language, as they're unique and clearly gifted. Let them be different; release the urge to judge or make them "fit in."

A big component of the bright magical souls is that they continually choose to live between two realms. The Unicorn Children are very much here on earth as well as on a magical dimension that is not of earth. Their ability to exist between the two realities keeps them connected to magic and soothes their souls. Sometimes when you look at them, they are indeed not really here; their eyes will be somewhere else. Nurture and honor that they live between two realities. It helps them to stay true to who they are by traversing at will between these places.

It is a true blessing to be in their presence. They melt your heart and heal your soul, igniting things that you did not know existed. It is simple: they do not need to use words or methods. Their power is in play, love, laughter, and peace. They remind all of us of this simple truth as they come to earth.

Integration is key. We are here to be integrated, to know ourselves, to believe in the purity that flows joyfully from within, and to allow it to be the foundation of our experience. The Unicorn Children bring this forth.

There are few words to describe these angelic souls of love. Their presence awakens and shifts your reality, allowing you to let go of concepts that separated you from your pure essence and bringing communion, creation, and alignment in its purest form.

Chapter 9

FOSTERING HARMONY WITH STAR CHILDREN

Here we discuss many powerful ways of creating space and opportunities for the new children to channel their energy, restore inner balance, and create peace within. These practices, activities, and skills are also very powerful and fun for adults.

It is important to allow the children to be exactly who they are, to teach, share, and demonstrate a new perspective. Set them free from caring about others' opinions by practicing this yourself. Show them that love is unconditional. As you allow your children to be free to be who they truly are, you also say yes to you by being who you authentically are. Ultimately, encourage yourself to expand and live from the space of the heart as love, nurturing the deepest, most joyful desires of your soul.

Love the children always, and show the way by example. It is okay to be different, to look different, to have new, innovative ideas, and to live outside the box. Believing in their unique authentic self is their biggest asset.

Tools for Harmony

Water

There is a cleansing and balancing element to water. Rain has a magical way of soothing one's soul and bringing new life to the world. Have you felt comforted by the sound of raindrops on the roof? Similarly, the ocean, rivers, streams, lakes, and even a bath or shower have a way of connecting us with our pure, happy state of being.

This is helpful for all of us. After a long day of working with clients, enjoying friends, going to school, or just having a fun afternoon, it's refreshing to take a shower or bath. As I've mentioned, every day after school, our son Luca takes a shower, which allows him to balance and to let go of anything he picked up as a highly sensitive, gifted soul; it allows him to be free to be himself. He is always so happy after his shower. It shifts everything, especially if he comes home not feeling like his typical happy-go-lucky, creative, dancing self. How do showers change your perspective in life?

Spending time in the ocean or near any natural source of water is a great way to connect. Many healing elements are at play when we are in nature. Have you ever sat beside a river and watched the water flow? Quickly, you enjoy the present moment, appreciating every miraculous element of the experience. Jumping into the ocean gives a similar feeling. As soon as you are completely submersed in the cold salt water, everything that is not naturally you falls away. You emerge smiling and feeling light. I love the ocean.

Create rituals that involve connecting with the water, while always sending love, gratitude, and blessings to Mother Earth and her running water. Your children will love this and for the rest of their days will honor the connection between the luscious elements of life on earth and how sweetly we support each other.

Food

You know how important it is to feed our bodies. It's instinctive and clear. Here we emphasize the importance of eating and honoring clean, pure, local, organic, whole foods. It is easy to nourish your body when you eat minimally processed foods. Eat what feels good. Cook at home as much as possible. Honor, thank, and connect with the ingredients as you create. Be grateful, and see how great you feel when nourishing your body and spirit with the final product.

Include your children and your inner child in the process of buying food. Feel the vibration as you make your selection. What draws you in and makes you feel alive? Are there certain things that feel harsh and that repel you? Consciously connect as you collect your ingredients. See how this changes your life.

Star Children are sensitive to foods and harsh chemicals. If your children experience intense irritability, skin rashes, irritated bowel tendencies, or stomachaches, tune in and connect with your children and their angels. Ask what you need to know and whether there are any foods you should remove from their diet. Listen and look for repeated signs, and trust the intuitive nudges you receive. For highly sensitive souls, consuming foods that their bodies do not know how to digest can cause much discomfort.

I have firsthand experience with a Star Child who has severe sensitivity to gluten. Luca has been allergic his entire life. I picked up on it early, when he was only breastfed. At the time I rarely ate gluten, and I realized that when I did, he would become sick within hours. As a seven-year-old Rainbow Child, he remains allergic to gluten. His reaction can be described as his being uncomfortable in his body. Everything becomes difficult; he throws tantrums, has outbursts, and resists simple things, like walking out the door. If this happens, we can easily identify that he has eaten gluten, and we understand and allow it to play out. His allergy has been confirmed with a genetic test. Some new children cannot digest the gluten proteins in certain grains. This is something to consider if your child exhibits similar behavior. Perhaps your child is sensitive to food coloring, sugar, dairy, soy, or eggs. Let this empower you on your journey of love.

Meditation

Meditation is a great way to connect with yourself in a deep, grounded, peaceful, and fulfilling way. It's an opportunity to go beyond the limited perception of the mind. It is an uplifting practice for people of all ages. Quickly, life becomes a meditative practice of presence, magic, and joy. In meditation, we connect with our breaths, unite with our hearts, receive divine guidance, and come to know that everything happens exactly as it needs to in the highest good for all.

My own deep desire to meditate was the catalyst for much of the healing, awareness, clarity, and alignment in my life. Meditating daily at the beginning and end of my day, as well as being guided throughout the day, is how I consciously began creating peace and true alignment on my earthly journey. It allowed me to go beyond the moment, to know that everything is flowing perfectly, and to see the hidden blessings. Allowing this time for myself in the midst of an overwhelming situation has been a great example for my children. They know if I am meditating that I am not available to respond to their questions; this allows me to truly honor my deep desire for peace and solitude, which is one way I love myself.

Creating a Meditation Sanctuary

Children love connecting in this peaceful, serene, quiet, and comforting way. Create a special place in your home, which I refer to as a sanctuary. It will be a go-to place to find stillness whenever your heart desires. Allow your children to choose a special object to place in this area. They may have a stone, feather, plant, or favorite furry pet animal friend that honors their space. Make sure you choose a quiet location, far from distractions. You may be guided to place a pillow nearby to sit on, and playing quiet music is a possibility.

Depending on the age and independence of your children, you may decide to sit and breathe with them the first few times or on your own. Meditation is an option for them to choose and explore. Your example and cocreation of this sanctuary is the most empowering action you can make. Let go, and leave it up to them. It is important that we never push our children into anything. This empowers them to create their own worlds and reminds them that they truly are miraculous.

Breath

You may wonder why I discuss such a simple concept. Breath is the life-force energy that runs through each and every one of us. It connects us to all life-forms, purity, creation, and harmony. When you're overwhelmed, breathe. Teach your children the power and importance of enjoying long, deep belly breathing. Be an example.

Center in Breath
Close your eyes and breathe.
Count for eight seconds while you inhale.
Hold your breath for eight seconds.
Exhale for eight seconds.
Repeat eight times.

It is okay if you don't complete this entire practice. The intention is to connect clearly with yourself.

Creative Expression

How our hearts long to create, make mistakes, learn, and try again. Activities that allow this in a playful, joyous, and expansive way are good for our hearts and souls. It doesn't matter how old or young we are. All of us are children at heart.

There are many wonderful options to explore: drawing, painting, using chalk, cutting, creating dream boards, making music, playing drums, dancing, collecting objects from nature and creating a collage, painting rooms, or decorating your home in a new and exciting way.

Feel Your Feelings

Encourage children to feel their feelings. Let them know that it is okay to experience uncomfortable emotions. Allow them to thoroughly express themselves through tears, words, and bodily movement. When we learn to self-soothe by repressing and ignoring our feelings, many negative results occur that create a lifetime pattern of resistance and deep-rooted pain.

Teach your children by example. Be honest with yourself when things get tough, and let go of the layers of resistance that have formed within you. To do this, you must feel through feelings of discomfort and release them. Once you have cleared and released your fears, hurt, or frustration, there will be openness and a light resonance within your heart. This is a powerful process of healing and saying yes to bliss. It is also something you can encourage children to do when they are overwhelmed and emotional.

Feel your feelings. Give little ones time and space to do this as well. Know that for them, it is a process, just as it is for you. Trust the process, and love them through the journey.

Movement

Physical activity is so important for these high-vibrational souls. It helps them to connect and release what is not truly theirs. Consider incorporating movement in any form. Perhaps your child enjoys being with others; if so, you might consider a class such as gymnastics, dance, or kids' yoga. There is a wide assortment of sports to consider as well. Another beautiful thing is to incorporate physical activity in your life and bring your children along for the fun.

At age seven, Luca loves joining me on runs. He brings his scooter and flies alongside me. I see a huge change in his personal level of joy and freedom when he is physically active. The same goes for me. My life is full of movement. It keeps me clear and aligned in my own unique energy.

Music

Music can make us feel relaxed or meditative. Making music welcomes us to enter a state of presence and awareness that is very joyful. I encourage you to gather percussion instruments—drums, maracas, rain sticks, a keyboard, even pots and spoons—to create a fun, festive environment with your family, and make your own rhythm to dance to.

Soothing meditative music is always great to have on hand. This simple tool sets the energy in your home, car, and life. When it is time to slow down, I play a wonderful, spirited flute CD. It puts my youngest right to sleep and fills our sanctuary with a loving vibration.

Music is also an uplifting form of expression. It assists Star Children in channeling their energy in a positive way. This is extra important to recognize because many of these souls have much more energy running through them than their parents. Positive outlets lead to increased harmony within, which you will notice quickly in your little ones.

Nature

In nature—walking, sitting, playing, meditating, or perhaps camping—everything feels different. After a nap under a tree or hike in the forest, colors look more vibrant. You'll notice peace and joy and a connection between every living element; you'll begin to glow. This is the balancing effect of nature. It nurtures our souls' natural essence, supporting us by holding a clear, safe space to connect and shine.

If you've had a long day or need a boost, walk along a trail in the forest or a nearby park, or find a welcoming tree to sit beneath. This is an excellent practice for all ages; animals benefit from this as well.

You will feel clear, peaceful, balanced and open to receiving intuitive messages in the forest, sea, and under a tree. This is because pure, loving energy is everywhere. Nature provides us with natural grounding as well as healing; plus, it's easy, free, fun, and feels so good.

Offer gratitude to Mother Earth and her plants, animals and sacred water as you enter and depart. You will notice they help and support you too. They also have messages for you. If you are open, say hello to the tree and ask whether there is something it wants you to know. Listen with your heart. Speak of the fairies and *Menehune*, which are the little people that inhabit and care for the plants. This practice is great to share with children and will change your experience as an adult too. It's fun to remind our kids that other worlds do exist.

Crystals, Gems, and Stones

There are unique healing and grounding properties to crystals, gems, and stones. These earth elements can easily be incorporated into our daily lives, assisting us by providing soothing, protective, healing components; clarity; and increased intuition, and they boost our connection with Source, among many other beautiful, blessed experiences.

It is lovely to have something tangible, such as a stone, with which to connect. Talking about the world of spirit can feel elusive at first. A sacred item, such as a crystal, can boost our confidence, provide something physical to relate to, and give us silent permission to go deeper, releasing old fears and truly allowing us (both adults and children) to embrace our joy of being deeply connected to who we are as we explore soul gifts, trust, and know everyone is safe. Love is who we are.

Enjoy exploring the world of crystals, stones, and gems. You may find a special gem outdoors or at a store, or you could be inspired to buy a book that teaches about their various properties. I encourage you to allow your intuition to guide you to the right one. It's fun to visit a rock store and pick a stone purely on what you are energetically attracted to. This is so powerful and honors the wisdom that is always flowing within you. You know what you need. You always have known, and you always will, especially when you are flowing and connected.

Connecting Exercises

My favorite exercise is a visualization and guided meditation. It taps souls into seeing, connecting with and learning to clear, align, and tune in to their own energy. This is a great tool for all ages. When kids are introduced to such easy and empowering techniques, they welcome a level of self-awareness that allows them to stay tapped into their individual magical essence. And as for adults, this reminds us of our own intrinsic abilities and gifts.

Expand as Light

Take a few deep breaths, close your eyes, tune in, and empty your energetic body.
Become a hollow, clear vessel with each breath, releasing and letting go completely.
Affirm, "I lovingly release all that is not mine."
Continue to breathe and release until your entire body feels empty.
Once you are clear, empty, and open, allow a golden vortex of Source/
love/universal energy to flow in, via your belly button.
Enjoy the crystalline, golden, warm, love energy as it ripples to every cell
of your being, filling you up as the pure being of love that you are.
With each inhalation, allow the energy to become
thicker, more powerful, potent, and vibrant.
Once you are filled and glowing, allow the light to seep outside of your
body, creating a pillow of light around you. With each inhalation, fill with
light; then, as you exhale, allow the light to flow from the inside out.
When you are ready, open your eyes.
This is you—a beautiful bubble of light. Enjoy!

Cleaning and Organizing

You can revitalize your life and release by cleaning and letting go of old things. This physical act honors where you are and is a powerful catalyst for internal change.

Clearing and releasing the old increases the energetic vibration of the space you inhabit. It's integral in moving forward. This process also creates a safe, happy place for you, your children, and the furry family members you may have.

When cleaning, I always thank my space, sending love and appreciation to everything and honoring the beautiful gifts that it provides. You may also light a candle, say a few words, burn sage or incense, clean your crystals, sing a song, whirl through the room, decorate, or rearrange the entire place.

Grounding

As in-tune, highly sensitive, intuitive beings who are connected and flowing with divine love, we are always in need of extra grounding to stay balanced and in harmony on earth.

There are many joyful ways to be in balance. Some of my favorite include dancing, yoga, hiking, hula-hooping, walking barefoot, gardening, digging in the mud (like kids do sometimes), cooking, running, and playing at the park (like a big kid, of course). These activities open, activate, and expand our root chakra, the part of our energetic being that feels safe, connected, and supported on earth.

Another powerful way to activate your root chakra, which is at the base of your pelvis and vibrates as the color red, is through meditation. You can focus on this part of your being as you invite and visualize your body as it roots into the earth, growing energetic extensions like the bold roots of a tree, truly anchoring into Mother Earth, and receiving the blessing of her refreshing, soothing, purifying presence. This will further allow you to connect, honor, and activate your grounded earthly existence in this lifetime—Star Children especially tend to need more of this in order to thrive.

Blessings, Honoring, and Gratitude

Blessings are all around us. As we walk outside, the earth supports and lifts us up; the sun nourishes our cells, providing light; and the air feeds our body with precious life-force energy. When we approach life as a blessing, we become conscious. As we give thanks and gratitude for all things, our appreciation grows. The connection we create with our world reminds us that support is always present.

You easily can integrate this experience with your children; they will love it and will remind you of this too. It's enjoyable and feels so good. Perhaps you start by thanking the ingredients in a recipe as you prepare it. Then as you sit to eat, you again thank and honor your food with love. The love you send to your food also increases its vibration and provides more nourishment for you and your loved ones.

A beautiful practice is to make offerings of gratitude or prayer. When I have flowers, I bring them to a special place, perhaps a river or tree I visit to rest and reset. I place the flowers as an offering, saying a few words of gratitude and honoring all the blessings I receive. Other times, I am guided to offer flowers, food, gemstones, or feathers as a way of releasing something that no longer serves my journey in the highest and best for all. As I leave my offering where I am guided, I set the intention. At times I also leave offerings of gratitude to my ancestors, who travel close to me, and magical beings, such as my unicorn friend, fairies, or the dragon creatures that love to visit. When we connect to the otherworld, it is easy to receive their help and guidance. They love appreciation just as much as humans do.

A mindful, open-hearted life ripples far and wide. You are the creator of your reality. Be thankful for the life you live. The life you live will thank you in return.

Bedtime Rituals

It is a powerful practice to have a bedtime ritual, especially for the children who see and sense spirits. You and your little ones can take a moment to invite the angels, a relative in spirit, a friend, or anything that resonates to join them. The presence of familiar souls provides an instant sense of safety and comfort. You may play relaxing music and provide a small light to brighten the room.

When children share their experiences of connecting with or seeing a spirit, it is important to listen and ask questions, as this gives them permission to explore deeper. It also assures them that they are safe in sharing such a vulnerable experience with you. Remind them that all souls come from love and that it is perfectly safe to connect with them. They simply are humans without bodies. When we feel comfortable in the presence of a spirit, fear disappears, and we are free to connect, learn, and share together.

When someone has a fearful experience, it is often because we believe the unknown is scary. Perhaps our little ones intuitively pick up on our fear. When we know a spirit can be trusted, our experience becomes one of trust too. Look at this in terms of interaction with humans. For instance, if we label certain people as angry, they tend to show up in our lives as angry. When we see those same people as gentle and loving, they walk with a gentle, loving presence. It is the same with spirit; we must see the highest truth in all beings. This is our purpose—to see beyond what the eye shows us.

See the love in all. Raise your vibration and allow all to rise in your presence. Simply living this truth gives us silent permission to drop our stories and rise into our purest form.

Chapter 10

CONNECTED TO COLLECTIVE CONSCIOUSNESS

As angels on earth, here to cleanse, heal, and bring harmony, love, and balance, the awake Star Children are tapped into the collective consciousness. This is important to emphasize and therefore has been honored with its own chapter. Children and awake adults can feel what is happening on a global level, which can be an overwhelming experience at times. As very high-vibrational beings of love light, our ability to release and heal for the masses is huge. We are here to do this.

It is important that you are aware of this so you can be there to hold the children in a safe space of love, peace, and acceptance when this occurs. I say *we* because you are very special, and the children, as you realize by now, are in your life to remind you of this, calling you forward to rise as your highest truth.

Many of us want answers; we want to fix things and make everything okay. Often the answer is in surrender, in knowing that everything is perfect, in allowing our children to be exactly where they are. Similarly, when we experience such things, surrender is powerful. Allow the dust to settle, release, and let happy harmony take over. Whether someone is throwing a fit, crying, shining, or just being, remember that we each are unique special beings.

As a parent, adult, and loved one, it can be heart-wrenching to witness children in a state of despair, loss, anger, or hurt. Your job is not to make everything better but to be available, present, and open as love. You are asked to hold a powerful space of love. So let go of everything your head is screaming, breathe, connect with nature, find your roots, and be grounded as love. Miracles unfold simply from your connectedness, faith, and inner peace—huge miracles.

Great changes are happening on earth now, and we are asked to stay positive and grounded in light, love, peace, and joy. When there is chaos in the world, don't feed it with negative energy. Instead, center in the truth of love. An old layer of egoic patriarchal control is melting; this is its last attempt to be powerful. You must stay centered in truth and live freely in abundant peace. All of us who exist in our hearts, energetically open and living the highest truth, have been called forth in the most powerful way to spread love energy, especially now, when the world needs it most. Do what your heart calls you to do, and simply know that existing in joy is healing for you, the gifted kids in your life, and the entire universe.

Of course, it is great to check in with your kids. Ask questions, see whether there is something going on, be a safe place for them to share, and really listen. If they have nothing to share, know that something bigger than you is happening. Honor where they are, be thankful that you are aware, say a prayer, and give thanks for this journey.

This is a prime opportunity for you to connect with your guidance—to meditate, go within, call on your angels for support, and ask for the clarity that is waiting for you. I must emphasize that you are here with a big mission and purpose. Your child knows this, and you know this. Perhaps you will be given a "job" by the universe; they may ask you to hold a space of love, to repeat a set of words that will assist in healing the planet, to connect with a loved one, or to start a daily practice in your own life. Listen to the messages as they come through. They may be in the form of repetitive thoughts, dreams, ideas, numbers, inspiration, or as clear as messages written right before you.

Uniting with the child within us is a journey of joy, expression, and truth. Be grateful, honor life, love the process, and have fun.

Chapter 11

LABELS: AUTISM, ADD/ ADHD, ASPERGER'S SYNDROME

Any type of label is limiting. Labels put us in a box with requirements, expectations, and ideals, which can cut us off from the abundant energy that flourishes within our hearts, spirits, and souls. As I allowed this sacred guide to be written through me, I was challenged by the classification of the different children, specifically the Indigo, Crystal, Rainbow, Dolphin, and Unicorn souls. I was gently guided that the breakdown is to empower and lift us up. Always allow openness for change and expansion beyond what has been described.

Today we witness the use of labels in many fields, such as education and medicine. The use can be empowering as well as limiting. I experienced the use of labels intensely during my nursing education. It is the use of labels that made me certain I could not practice as a nurse, for I knew that these labels were the exact thing that kept people from uniting with their true perfection. Humans do not need medication, surgery, or treatment. The answers are within. We are the healers, the vehicles that decide what we are going to experience, when we will leave this planet, and how we want to live.

As I completed my bachelor's degree in nursing, I knew I could not practice within this scope of healing. My purpose is to remind souls of who they really are and why they are here, to connect them with these messages, to empower everyone to live fully united with their highest essence, and to lift blinders of separation and activate the reality of oneness that thrives deep within our souls.

My personal experience with labels is powerful. It gave me permission to walk the path of the unknown, following truth, and trusting beyond what I believed was a safe, secure path in life. I was walking on the edge, and I knew what I had to do. This moment was the beginning of the rest of my life.

Labels such as ADD, ADHD, autism, and Asperger's syndrome describe the children of today, the awake Star Children. They are different and don't fit in the box. The box I speak of refers to the general beliefs that society promotes and that many choose to live.

The awake Star Children represent change. They are love—creative forces that show a new way, reminding us of our essence and why we are here, and giving silent permission to create a new reality. I am a Star Child. I have found the way, the truth, and the passion in my heart as I say yes to the essence of my soul. Can you feel the ripple in your soul? This is why I am here.

I am going to share a powerful story of a mom named Kristine and her journey with her son, Jacob, who was diagnosed with autism at age two. Kristine was given a grim diagnosis and told to expect that Jacob would never talk. She instantly disregarded the diagnosis and followed her instincts, knowing in her heart that Jacob was perfect. She filled his world with anything in which he was even slightly interested, rather than focusing on what he could not do. Below is an excerpt written by Kristine.

> He liked repetitive behaviors. He would play with a glass and look at the light, twisting it for hours on end. Instead of taking it away, I would give him fifty glasses, fill them with water at different levels and let him explore. I surrounded him with whatever he loved.

The more she did that, the more it worked. Then one night, as he was being tucked in, Jacob spoke. "It was like music … because everybody had said it was an impossible thing," Kristine recalls. "I would tuck him in every night and say, 'Good night, baby Jacob. You're my baby angel and I love you very much.' One night he looked me straight in the eyes and said, 'Night-night, baby bagel.' All along he must have thought I had been calling him a bagel!"

Jacob is now a student of theoretical physics at the Perimeter Institute in Waterloo, Ontario, with an IQ measured as higher than Einstein's.

This is a fascinating example of how labels and expectations have a big impact on the outcome, experience and ability for us to be who we really are.

As a parent, teacher and advocate for Star Children, I suggest you remove all labels. Look at the child. What do they love? What are they trying to say? How can you nurture their gifts, listen more fully, and be entirely present? See them as the teachers. Take off your label as a parent, psychologist, teacher, auntie, and "adult," and join heart to heart in the moment. You will be amazed at what the children show you.

Chapter 12

CHILDHOOD ILLNESS

This is a hard topic to discuss when we think of children, but it is real, and we must honor and explore why the current generation of Star Children face illness at a very young age. The high-vibrational souls coming in have chosen to be conduits of healing and awakening on earth for the masses and, specifically, for their immediate loved ones. They transmute fear, change old stories, and force people to go beyond the limiting perspectives that have created their reality for a lifetime.

The children will do what it takes to accomplish their purpose. This can mean a number of things; it is different for each circumstance. Sometimes it takes a big wake-up call for people to *stop* the blind, unconscious flow that they are living. What would make any parent stop and reexamine life? Yes, the discomfort, pain, and unthinkable loss of a child.

We see, hear, and know of many families that experience this awful, heart-wrenching journey. I am here to share that this is an invitation to go beyond, seek truth, find alignment, and open to the messages of your soul. The answer is quite simple, and healing is always 100 percent possible, no matter what you are told the odds are. The children do not have to leave the planet to achieve their goal, but they will, if that is what it takes.

You have the power within you to make it through hard times, and your children do too. They can do it. The medical system is so matter-of-fact and frank. The truth is that a diagnosis, lab results, or answers (or lack of answers) from a medical perspective don't matter. You don't need any of this. It can make you believe things are worse than they are and create more fear, which hinders healing and the alignment that is accessible to you at all times.

Your number-one job is to go beyond what you see, hear, and think. Move into a space of letting go, and expand into wholeness. The messages will come, and the healing is there. Of course, if you need to get tests, treatment, and medical intervention, then do what makes you feel assured. This is simply a reminder of your magical ability as a healer to go beyond the physical and tap into the pure power of your being. I am reminding you that everything is possible.

My heart goes out to those of you who have witnessed your children return to spirit. I am humbled by the strength you have. My heart holds you in the deepest place of love. I am sorry. You have done nothing wrong. Release yourself from guilt. Know that your angels are at peace and that they are right by your side now, holding your hand, hugging you, and lifting you when you're weary. Everything happens for a reason. In time, you will begin to heal, and clarity will make its way through the heavy rainclouds. I am with you, and so are your angels. Ask the divine for support when you need it, and watch as it appears in magical, unexpected ways.

All of the children are special. You are special, and you too are very much a child at heart. Love yourself; be an example. Listen to your heart. Allow changes, and be open to more greatness than you ever knew possible.

Chapter 13

MISCARRIAGE

Y ou may have firsthand experience with the loss of an unborn child or know someone who has. Often, this experience leaves many questions, open-heart wounds, and a great sense of loss. I invite you to journey beyond the very real experience of losing a child and into a place of welcoming the transformation that it ignites.

This experience invokes emotion—intense, deep, connected emotion. It asks you what you really want and leaves many questions in its path. I write this chapter as a mother who lost three babies before they were born, each time with important messages: healing and clarity.

The Star Children are good at making sure that everything is aligned before their arrival. One way to do this is to pop into the physical but then leave quickly. This invites expecting parents to dig deep, feel, and heal that which has been buried deep inside.

Another aspect of miscarriage and Star Children is that these souls are not used to the very dense energetic vibration on earth. It can take them a few attempts to integrate and fully come into physical form here. Each time they enter the womb is a step forward, and the next time, it is easier. This is not to say that all Star Children enter in stages, but some do, and it's important to create awareness about this.

As I write this, I sit joyfully pregnant, thirty weeks along, and excited to birth another Star being. The journey that led me here was not simple. I experienced two consecutive miscarriages prior to this pregnancy, one just months after the other. I share this because I know that many people experience this. You need to know you must keep the faith, listen to your intuition, and trust what you know deep within your heart.

During this pregnancy, the soul in my belly has asked not to be seen by the doctor and that I trust and allow it to grow happily on its own, as it does not need outside assistance. This is my third child and a completely new experience. I trust and feel the kicks as it happily moves about, and I follow the guidance I receive. I do feel that if I'd gone to the doctor, this child would have miscarried as well. This was a lesson for me to truly listen to the guidance and live completely in the allowing of truth that flows within. It is tantalizing and joyful to be here in this moment. And so I trust, allow, and continue to expand in bliss.

I understand, to an extent, what other women have gone through as they move through different stages of acceptance and loss. The blessing in this experience has always been the messages from both spirit and my baby. At the time of my last miscarriage, the soul said she would be back soon and that she was working with other "stars"—this is what she called the unborn children on the same mission as her: to complete healing on earth and make sure that everything is aligned. She came in and told me this mission had been completed, and I was pregnant again within days.

I have had the misery of releasing the physical fetal body, embracing the fact that I was not immediately going to have a new Star Child in my life to enjoy, nurture, and laugh and play with. Sadness set in, so many tears released, and acceptance that anything is possible would eventually land. My process involved sitting in stillness, without answers, emotions, or thoughts. In magical time, my soul opened, ready for the next chapter. I knew all was well and was once again excited and grateful for this experience.

Misdiagnosed miscarriage is quite common in early pregnancy, especially among the Star Children, as they develop in their own time, and sometimes their souls are off on a mission while in utero. I experienced what looked like, on the outside, a miscarriage, complete with lots of red blood, around eleven weeks. Spirit guided me to trust, rest, and stay home for several days. My guides told me to retreat into the forest for healing, connection, and alignment. Instead of visiting the doctor this time, I trusted and surrendered to what the universe would bring as I held the most powerful space of love from within. I nurtured my soul, listened, expanded, and knew all was well.

I am so grateful to have this connection with truth, to trust and listen. I credit this process with the birth of my third Star Child, who, coincidently, is named Star. So much gratitude overflows through my soul for this journey.

Every time I experienced a miscarriage there were profound openings, messages, and lots of clarity. The sorrow of the loss was washed away as the next chapter opened. It is so important to keep hope, feel your feelings, and remain open to joy.

I share my experience with you, as many Star Children clearly integrate on the earth plane in steps. They help to align the world they will enter by coming and going, if necessary, opening your heart wide, and clearing any old clutter that needs to be released. Know that there is a spiritual message behind all of your experiences and that a hidden blessing is waiting to be seen. I invite you to welcome the hidden blessings in your life.

Chapter 14

HONORING YOUR SACRED SPACE

Children ask for our attention, answers, time, energy, and commitment. They look to us for guidance, approval, assurance, respect, safety, and acceptance as they watch our every move to see how they should operate in the world. Being a parent can be the hardest, best, most demanding experience. It is the most rewarding job that never ends.

The key to success is to love yourself; this is for everyone. Step back from the demands of life, your child, your career, family obligations, and such, and determine what you need. Then say yes to allowing this in your reality.

Activity: What Are My Heart, Soul, Spirit, Mind, and Body Asking For?

Take a moment to meditate on this. Create an intention to clearly understand what you need for the highest and best for you and all that ripples from your roots.

You will need the following:
- a quiet place
- a piece of paper or a journal
- pens, markers, or crayons
- ten minutes

Find a quiet place, away from the distractions of life, and close your eyes. Breathe. Inhale and exhale for a full minute, until everything slows down and you unite with your center. This is a peaceful place of unconditional love. It is quiet, calm, and joyful.

Now ask, "What do I need right now for myself? Show me how to move forward in a way that invites me to be joyfully present and whole."

Sit, embracing long, deep breaths. Feel the emotions, thoughts, feelings, and sensations as they arise. Notice, forgive, and let go. Now you are clear, centered, and open to receiving the guidance that exists abundantly within.

Use this creative, intuitive process as you are guided. Sometimes you may want to color, draw, write, or simply breathe through the exercise. Once you feel the experience is complete, thank and honor yourself, your angels, guides, ancestors, and all the teachers of love and light who have shared their wisdom.

Be aware throughout your day of any ideas, thoughts, or messages. They are answers to the prayers that you placed in the universe. Be open and receptive to the love, joy, peace, and abundance that flow from this beautiful practice of going within and honoring all that is.

Chapter 15

CONNECT WITH YOUR HIGHEST SELF

There is energy of separateness, authority, and the need to be heard and respected on planet Earth. It moves souls into an element of separating from their highest essence, which is always love. The need to be in control causes an experience of lack, ownership, resentment, and disconnection from the present moment, which is life in its full form.

Many children experience this. Their environment may feel angry and overwhelming, causing them to rebel and even say things that are not in their true nature. This is because, in essence, they are not aligned with their highest selves. Instead, they have attuned with the energy of the environment and have forgotten who they are for a moment, several minutes, or possibly longer.

Living a life that is true to your heart's essence, soul energy, and spirit is powerful. Creation is your job, and your number-one responsibility is to shine brightly as who you really truly are. When you feel that you have lost touch, take time for yourself. You may be guided to go on a solo vacation, take an afternoon to connect in nature or even a few minutes to breathe, be in silence, meditate, take a bath, or enjoy a nap.

This is true for children as well. When they act in an unusual manner, give them the opportunity to connect with themselves.

Here is a list of activities that support our children in uniting with themselves:

- playing in nature
- swimming in the ocean or a pool
- taking a bath
- listening to or creating joyful, uplifting music
- cleaning and clearing their space
- allowing emotions to flow and be expressed through tears, words, or on paper as art
- stopping and breathing
- hugging a tree

As parents, we can model aligning behavior when we experience similar emotions or experiences. It is great for us to be open and honest about these experiences, first with ourselves and then with our children. It will comfort them to know that we also go through moments of being overwhelmed. It creates a stronger connection, and the authentic vulnerability provides an opportunity to clear energy as well as emotions.

When children experience such self-expressive moments, we can take a second to tap into our divine guidance, and create the environment or an opportunity that best suits their needs at that particular moment in time. We are here to support one another. Just as we are interested in the highest and best for our children, they also are interested in the best for us. They are happy to see us thrive. Our happiness makes them shine too.

Realize that the environment does not dictate what you will experience. The key is to always be centered in love and express your spirit in the fullest form. When you fly as the abundant energy you are, love is all you see.

Chapter 16

LIVING FROM THE
HIGH HEART

To wake up often means allowing your life to shift and your perspective to expand so that you live in alignment with your highest soul expression. We experience many expectations, ideas, and structures from the moment of entrance into this world. Often, our *knowing* is flooded, thus becoming clouded and confused. We come to a point of losing touch with our true essence and life mission.

I experienced this and have witnessed many others walking through life, fulfilling the expectations of society, family, peers, or their egos. We cannot be happy, however, until we live from the space of our pure, open, expanded heart. It does not matter what we do as long as we are connected and living from the part within us that is caring, loving, and purposeful. Our hearts truly allow us to be who we are. Let's explore the concept of our hearts and how to live from this space.

The energy we hold within our hearts dictates our entire experience. If our hearts are wide open, receptive, and loving, we share, receive, and experience this wherever we are. If our hearts are hard as stone, we will emit and receive this same experience. It is extremely important for us to tap into the energy of our hearts to see, feel, release, and open this sacred space.

If we are scared, fearful, hurt, or intimidated, our hearts may be covered with shields. When we exist in a space of love, trust, and honor, our hearts are open and receptive to both giving and receiving. Tapping into, acknowledging, opening, and clearing the space of our hearts is an important practice in our daily lives.

Touching Your Heart Meditation

Close your eyes. Breathe, enjoying several long, deep, clearing, centering belly breaths. As you exhale, let everything go. As you inhale, fill with divine white light. When you feel centered, clear, and at peace, move to step 2.

Call in your divine guides of love and light, your angels, the ascended masters, your highest self, ancestors, Source, and anything you are guided to connect with at this time to assist in the expansion of your heart. Release all that no longer serves you, and receive divine messages and clarity; awaken your heart and trust yourself.

Focus your energy on the chakra center of your heart (center of your chest). See the vibration; feel the emotion. Is the energy solid, thick, tight, tense, at ease, open, or light? Do you see a color, feel a texture, or sense an emotion? Many descriptions will resonate. Allow yourself to feel what is present in this particular moment for you. Remember you are the healer.

Move your attention from the surface of your heart to the core. Allow yourself to consciously move into the center of your heart space. What do you see, feel, and perceive? Become aware of your heart space. Ask questions as you notice things, and release.

You have gained insight, messages, and a sense of what you are experiencing in this moment. Now listen to your heart. What does it need? Why is it feeling this way? Listen. Trust your intuition, and allow.

Allow the stories, fears, limitations, and desires to gently fall away. You may see a layer melt from your heart, hardness disappear, or light fill it up. Breathe. It's possible you will discover objects or clutter in this space. Allow it to be cleared. As you breathe, call in your angels and highest self to assist you in releasing all that no longer serves you in the highest good for all. Continue to breathe, and be in this still, connected space until your heart is empty, clear, open, and at peace.

Now fill the space of your heart with light. You may add sparkles, love, sunlight, a seashell—anything you are inspired to place in this precious and open space of who you are.

Enjoy, and take a moment to smile. Acknowledge the way you feel, and *shine*. This is who you really are.

Thank the universe and all of the divine helpers who assisted you.

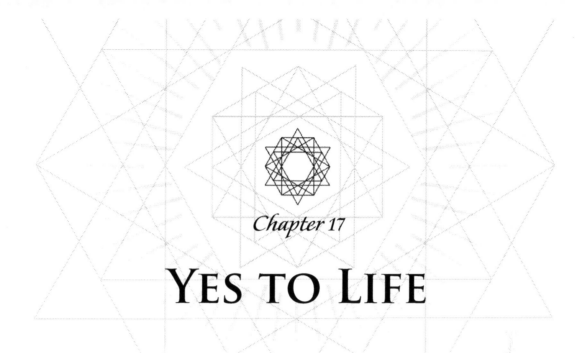

Chapter 17

YES TO LIFE

The reason we are all here is to shine, to be our authentic selves, and to walk authentically in truth, no matter what crosses our paths. We are peaceful warriors of love, light, and joy. The children and the child within each of us show us the way, teaching from a space of purity and leading us forward as pure, passionate bliss.

You have an inner child; this is the part of you that was vividly alive during childhood; the energy within your being that is carefree, open, excited, loving, tender, sweet, alive, and curious. Too often, our inner children experience circumstances that cause them to contract in fear, pain, and resistance. This leads us forward on a restricted journey until we are able to touch that part of ourselves that was hurt. We then listen to it, hear what it has to say, and release worries that have been harbored, healing our emotional, energetic body. What does your inner child have to share with you?

Meditate on This

Close your eyes, and enjoy several deep breaths.
You may be guided to speak with your inner child. Draw, write, lie down, and receive while in a dreamlike state, or enjoy a silent walking meditation. Follow your intuitive guidance by doing what feels right to you in this moment.

Creation

The next step is to realize that you are the sole creator of your life. This is such an important, powerful truth. It is the key to success and what the children are here to teach and remind us. Have you experienced a time when children dug their heels in the ground, refusing to listen to your commands? They were reminding you that when something or someone is not coming from a space of love, there is no need to listen. Today's children stand firm in what they "know" to be the truth, and they are setting great standards for you.

What do you do when children decide that you are not worthy of their reaction? Do you raise your voice and threaten them, deciding to take something away or punish them for not adhering to you? Maybe they are too consumed in their own world to even listen. Then what? Perhaps you read between the lines and take this as a sign to *stop* and breathe, to welcome your inner sanctuary into the experience, and let go of your schedule, desires, and agenda. As you enter this space that is pure within yourself, you may experience emotions such as anger, sadness, relief, or resentment. Breathe through this experience, and welcome the emotion. As you allow each feeling to surface with awareness, recognize it and love it.

Know deep inside that the children have everything within them to get through this. Be a safe presence by their sides, a pinnacle of love. Soon, the emotions will stop flowing, and you will open to experience a lull in thoughts, the presence of love, and a fullness of self-forgiveness. Sometimes a message or clarity appears for you—one of peace and understanding—that allows complete freedom and welcomes a new way. You now approach challenging moments in a way that lifts everyone up in the rising energy of love, honor, respect, and freedom.

Children invite these experiences as much as we do. We chose to be their parents and asked for a life of greater joy, importance, and abundance. They are here because we welcomed them. Now they teach exactly what we are ready to learn. It is important to recognize the great connection between the experiences we have and the opportunity each holds.

We can live in infinite ways. In each moment, we have the ability to choose love or fear. Love is expansive, and often, at the beginning, it pushes us into areas with which we are not completely comfortable. It requires us to remove protective barriers and live raw, open-hearted lives. Moving beyond our comfort zones allows us to learn, receive, and be who we are on a deeper level than we even knew existed. It does require us to move outside the box of being "safe." Unfamiliar territory is the place where we create miracles. It is the cusp of our existence and the point at which we will know no end.

Faith

You know when you are on the right path and can see beyond the limits that have been claimed as real too many times in this world. You just *know*. The children do too. They have more faith than you will ever believe. This is how they operate—from a space of pure faith. I see faith as knowing and believing, with no room for doubt. Move beyond believing and welcome the roar within your soul to honor the highest truth, your abilities, your purpose, your worthiness, and your soul. Now open your wings and *fly*.

Faith has brought me to this point in my life; it has allowed me to step into my truth, write this book, teach, learn, share, be a powerful messenger of love, heal and align, and show a new way. I credit faith for so much; it allows us to move beyond what we once believed as true and into a new concept as we shed old ideas and ways of being that never truly honored who we are.

I ask you to live wholeheartedly with faith, to trust yourself, and to know that there is great power within each of us.

Chapter 18

EXPAND AS YOU

This is why you are here. It is why *you* are alive, and it feels so good!

As the sun rises, we are reminded of new beginnings, of the ability to forgive deeply, and to let go of old stories. We are given the gift of new life with each breath. This tender opportunity often goes unnoticed. I invite you to start fresh and notice these moments. If things feel heavy, tedious, or off balance, step back and create the space you need to unite with your inner self. Pull your car over near a tree, walk outside barefoot, and sit on the earth. Close your eyes and enjoy several long, releasing breaths with loud exhalations. Enjoy this moment, and be free.

It is time to be at peace, to release the stories that brought you here into the infinite timeless universe. This moment is when you decide to birth the highest version of you. It's your decision. What will you decide? I hear your highest essence saying loud and clear, "*You* are a diamond, here to *shine*!" This is why you are here.

Ceremony of Renewal

Create a safe place for yourself, much like when you are about to meditate—cozy, clear, inviting, and honoring. You may want to be alone or invite your children to join in this loving creation. Be guided.

Light a candle, and as you do, silently set an intention. Bring a soft blanket to sit on or wrap around you. Bring your favorite beverage, and if you are guided, bring stones, play soft music, or have a beautiful piece of paper and pen nearby.

Invite all of you—your highest self, your inner child, your soul from many walks of life—to join and show you what needs to be released in honor of your heart, spirit, and whole essence so that you are free to live, love, and expand blissfully from this moment on.

Sit quietly, breathe deeply, close your eyes, and observe. Emotions, stories, people, thoughts or feelings with words, and messages may pass through your awareness. Listen, allow, trust, and feel. This is a cleansing time for everything to release. Allow yourself to go deep. Take your time, and be brave. Breathe, and allow the process to unfold until all is calm, and nothing further comes up for review.

Now say, "I lovingly release all that does not serve the highest and best." Enjoy a deep breath, and close your eyes. Allow yourself to become an empty vessel inside; visualize the energy from every cell of your body clearing out and releasing, starting from the top of your head, all the way down through your fingers and toes. Continue to breathe until you feel completely clear and light.

Now connect and fill with the energy of Source, which is the pure, positive vibrant, white-light energy—exactly the same essence as who you are, where you came from, and what supports your inner peace and nourishment while expanding your soul. This is *you*. Invite Source energy, in the form of crystalline white light, to fill you from the top of your head, allowing it to pour into every cell of your being. Feel warmth, joy, love, and peace exude from within as you welcome this life-force energy. With each breath, allow the light to grow. Once you feel light flowing through your entire being as you exhale, let this light expand through the pores of your skin, creating a beautiful sphere of your energy around you. Continue this for several breaths; inhale light, and then exhale, feeling your inner light as it expands from the inside out.

As you consciously cultivate and witness your energetic bubble of love growing, have fun with it. You can let it grow large, filling the entire room, and then bring it back in to be as big as your body or small as a seed. I typically enjoy ending this ritual with my energetic bubble expanding about a foot around my physical body.

This practice is nurturing and nourishing. It is a way of honoring you and is a great tool to stay centered in your own divine energy. I highly recommend starting every day with meditation, connecting with your highest self, giving gratitude, receiving clarity, and nurturing your heart, spirit, and soul.

As Star Children and parents of the special Star Children here on earth, this is the most important thing we can do for ourselves and the ones we love. It is time to say yes to you. It is time to be free, to know you are safe, and to trust your expansion as the beautiful soul you are and always have been.

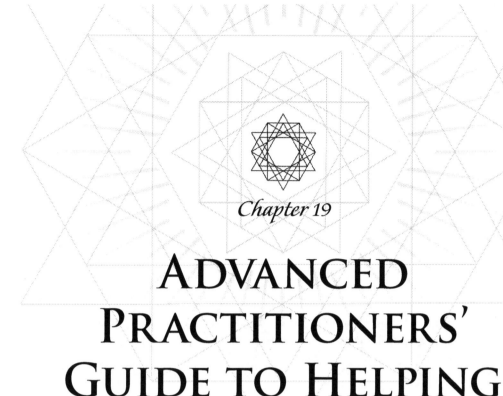

Chapter 19

ADVANCED PRACTITIONERS' GUIDE TO HELPING STAR CHILDREN

Many of you are here to uplift Star Children who have taken on big transmutation tasks. Often, they experience imbalance in their physical bodies as they shift big energies out of the consciousness of earth. How can you, as a practitioner or energy worker, assist them in restoring their innate balance and wholeness?

The first step is to ensure that you are balanced in your wholeness before attempting to help. Once you are, then you can proceed. The second step is to connect to their souls, their highest essence, and your guides as well as theirs. What are you shown right away? Allow your psychic, intuitive, clairvoyant gifts to reveal what is happening with the situation you are called to illuminate. Look, watch, hear, and feel. Ask questions when you are shown one thing so that you fully understand the situation and can assist. You are the observer, putting the pieces together.

What might be happening? The child likely is transmuting a false belief—an old concept that the world or a loved one holds—assisting a spirit, or being tapped into by a spirit. Independent of what is going on, the child needs to connect with their soul essence, source energy, the light that they are. If you are an advanced practitioner, you will see what is occurring on a higher level. When you see the whole story, you can clear and realign truth, in its highest vibrational essence, to ripple outward, freeing the child and all involved.

On a physical level, transmutation can be witnessed as a fever, cold, cancer, anger, sadness, or needing time alone. There is no need to jump to conclusions; always stay in an informed, connected relationship to what is happening. Your inner light is always more potent and powerful than anything that presents as fear.

It is your job to use your authentic, shiny, powerful vision and energetic skills to remind others of their innate wholeness and magic. This includes humans, spirit, or extraterrestrials joining from other planets. It is simple; when souls forget the magic within, they easily can experience a brainwashing, mind-control energy. On a basic psychic level, you will see and feel this energy occurring.

You can ask spirit what is the core of this, as well as asking how you clear and realign it in the highest and best for all. You are a wise one. This is *big* work that will heal our planet and her children. Love will change the world.

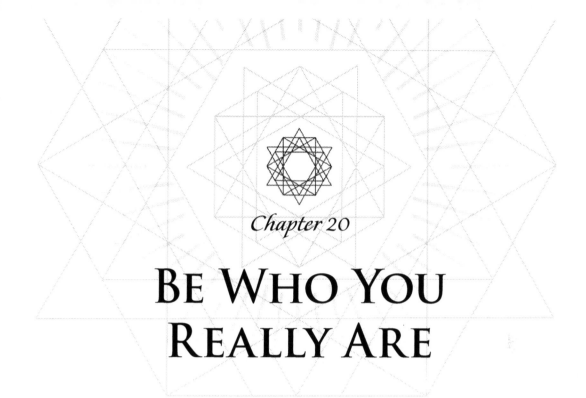

Chapter 20

BE WHO YOU REALLY ARE

I t is time for you to walk gently on momma earth, to care deeply, and to know yourself, your soul, your essence, and the love that supports you on this incredible journey. Your age, sex, location—all of the details are insignificant. *You*, the gem of this life, have been waiting to be seen, to blossom, to open. Claim your authentic path on this journey.

If you deeply love a child, know that child is helping you to align with this, your soul mission. In the end, it is about you and awakening your truest, highest self, your inner child, your gifts, your uniqueness and saying yes to your pure soul essence.

Everything that led to this moment in time has opened up a brand-new chapter within you. The readiness for change is undeniable. You felt the shifting beneath the surface, and saying yes is clearly the only way. I congratulate you for being here, for showing up and seeing yourself. The world is a beautiful place with you in it. You came here with a mission, a divine purpose, and it is *big*. You would not be reading these words otherwise; I promise.

The next step is to take action in little ways or big ways. Make life-changing choices that allow you to be happy, creative, and fully supported. You may experience criticism or fear from loved ones who think you've lost it, or you may experience your own doubts creeping in. Know your truth, claim it, take action.

There is nothing to wait for. Life is now, and you are here to live! It is with great honor, love, and joy that I say goodbye until we unite again. I am here with you always in spirit. Feel the love and support from your angels, ancestors, and divine guides of light. Let them lead you forward and clear the way when you need help. Call them in and be supported. I love you.

Printed in the United States
by Baker & Taylor Publisher Services